MEGAFAST PLANES

Thanks to the creative team:

Senior Editor: Alice Peebles

Design: www.collaborate.agency

First published in Great Britain in 2015
by Hungry Tomato Ltd
PO Box 181
Edenbridge
Kent, TN8 9DP

A CIP catalogue record for this book is
available from the British Library.

ISBN 978-1-910684-30-6

Printed and bound in China

Discover more at
www.hungrytomato.com

MEGAFAST PLANES

by John Farndon
Illustrated by Mat Edwards and Jeremy Pyke

HUNGRY
TOMATO™

CONTENTS

Introduction   6

That Was How Fast?!   8

Space Streaker   10
Darpa Falcon HTV-2 glider

Black Lightning   12
NASA's X-43A

Rocket Speed   14
X-15 rocket plane

Whistling through the Skies   16
Lockheed SR-71 Blackbird

Fox on the Run   18
MiG-25 Foxbat

Faster than Sound   20
Bell X-1

Supersonic Luxury   22
Concorde and the TU-144

Whirling Propellers   24
F8F Bearcat and World War II fighter planes

Sky racers   26
Air racing

Super Chopper   28
Eurocopter X^3

Want to Know More?   30

Index and Glossary   32

MEGAFAST PLANES

If you want to go truly megafast, you have to fly. Up in the air, there is very little to get in your way. An ordinary airliner flies at 500 mph or more. But even airliners are left far behind by some of the scarily fast planes featured in this book. Many of these aerial speedsters can streak through the sky at thousands of miles an hour. That's so much faster than sound that you only hear them coming long after they've whizzed past! So fasten your seat belt and prepare to have your breath taken away!

The Eurocopter X^3 is the world's fastest helicopter.

PRIVATE JET

Most of the world's fastest planes are used for military purposes. But if you're megarich you can still fly very fast in a Cessna Citation X: the world's fastest passenger plane. It can only carry 12 people, but it slices through the air at over 700 mph, close to the speed of sound.

JETMAN

You don't need a plane to fly fast. How about a personal jet pack you just strap to your back, then zoom off? Astronauts use jet packs in space. With hydrojet packs you can whoosh up over the sea or a lake on high-powered jets of water to perform acrobatic tricks (above). And Swiss inventor Yvès Rossy added wings to four jet packs to fly past jet airliners at speeds of up to 186 mph.

THAT WAS HOW FAST?!

It is easy to see when a plane or a bike, or a car or truck is megafast. But how do you know just how fast it is? Speed is the distance that something moves in a certain time. It is the distance covered divided by the time. If a jet plane travels 2,000 miles in two hours, it travels 1,000 miles in each hour. So we say its speed is 1,000 miles per hour or mph. The top speeds for the machines in this book are given in mph.

SPEED MATTERS

Speeds for vehicles on the ground are usually given in mph (miles per hour) or km/h (kilometres per hour). Rockets may soar away from Earth at over 11 km per second. If a plane flies faster than sound (typically over 700 mph), its speed may be compared to the speed of sound in similar conditions. This speed is called a Mach number. So a plane flying at the speed of sound is said to be flying at Mach 1, at 20 times the speed of sound it's Mach 20, and so on.

GETTING QUICKER

One way of seeing how fast something moves is to measure how quickly it gains speed – that is, its acceleration. You can actually measure how much something accelerates every second. But with fast vehicles, the acceleration is usually given by how long it takes to reach a particular speed, typically from a standing start, 0 mph. The shorter the time, the faster the acceleration. So acceleration figures for a superbike that takes just 2.9 seconds to get from a standstill to 60 mph would be: 0-60 in 2.9 seconds. That's megafast!

AGAINST THE CLOCK

The most accurate way of measuring top speed is to measure how long a vehicle takes to cover an exact distance, such as a mile. That's how the official top speeds in this book were measured. To ensure split second accuracy, the clock is triggered to start and stop when the vehicle cuts through a beam of light.

SPEED DIAL

Speed against the clock is average speed. Police speed guns and speedometers in cars, trucks and bikes register the speed at any one instant. Speed guns fire a radar beam, and detect the way it bounces back off the moving vehicle. With speedometers, an electronic sensor counts the number of times small magnets on the wheel sweep past it each second, and converts this into a speed in mph to display on a dashboard or LCD screen.

SPACE STREAKER

Imagine travelling from New York to Los Angeles in 12 minutes. Or round the world in less than two hours. That's how fast the Darpa Falcon HTV-2 rocket-launched glider can fly. It has to be carried very high in the air by a rocket before gliding back to Earth, and it is still an experimental project. But on 11th August 2011, it reached a mind-blowing 13,000 mph before crashing.

Top Speed	200	3400	6800

Protective launch shell

Minotaur IV Lite rocket launcher

POWER
None (as a glider)

LAUNCH SYSTEM
Minotaur IV Lite rocket (see left)

TOP SPEED
13,000–17,500 mph

MACH SPEED
20

LAUNCH ALTITUDE
100 miles

FLIGHT PLAN

Like a spacecraft, the HTV-2 was carried up into space inside the nose of a rocket, which was launched from Vandenburg Air Force base in California. Then high above the Pacific, the rocket's nose opened to release the glider, which flew back to Earth at hypersonic speeds.

SMASHING SOUND

A plane that flies faster than the speed of sound is said to be 'supersonic'. But when it flies more than five times faster than sound, it is called 'hypersonic'. HTV stands for Hypersonic Technology Vehicle – and HTV-2's flight was 20 times faster than the speed of sound! It was so fast that temperatures on the glider's body reached 3,500°F (1,926°C) in its three-minute flight – so hot that its skin disintegrated, which is why it crashed.

10200	13600	17000	17,500 mph

BLACK LIGHTNING

NASA's X-43A was the fastest powered plane... ever. Like the HTV-2, the X-43A was an experimental plane launched from mid-air that flew only once. Three X-43As were built. The first failed in mid-flight. The second shattered the world speed record for a jet plane in 2001, reaching 5,000 mph. The third was released 15 miles up in 2004, and screeched through the air at over 7,000 mph!

ROCKET-LAUNCHED

It's not easy launching an X-43A. It's attached to the Hyper-X booster rocket and carried high up in the air by a B-52 bomber. Eight miles up, the B-52 releases the booster rocket. In a matter of seconds, the rocket shoots the X-43A a further 12 miles up. Finally, the rocket falls away to leave the X-43A to make its high-speed flight.

Top Speed	200	3400	6800

SCRAMJET POWER

The X-43A is powered through the air by a Supersonic Combustion Ramjet, or Scramjet for short. Unlike conventional jets, which have fan blades to draw in air and compress it, scramjets have no moving parts. Instead, air is simply scooped up and rammed into the engine as the plane flies forward at supersonic speeds. Inside the engine, this supersonic rammed air is ignited with fuel to produce the engine's mighty thrust (see diagram below).

POWER
Scramjet

LAUNCH SYSTEM
B-52 plane

TOP SPEED
7,000 mph

MACH SPEED
9.65

LAUNCH ALTITUDE
20 miles

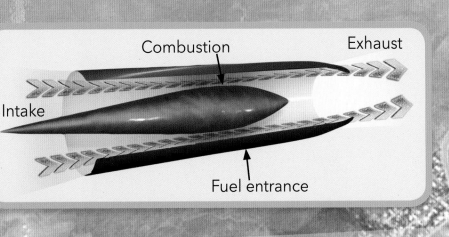

Combustion

Exhaust

Intake

Fuel entrance

10200	13600	17000	7,000 mph

ROCKET SPEED

Both the HTV-2 and the X-43A were unmanned aircraft. The highest and fastest-ever piloted flights were achieved in X-15 rocket planes. In 1963, pilot Joseph Walker twice took an X-15 more than 65 miles up to the very edge of space. This was so high that it qualified him as an astronaut! Four years later, Pete Knight screeched through the air in an X-15 at a blistering world record speed of 4,520 mph!

FLYING HIGH

Like the X-43A, the X-15 was carried high into the sky by a big B-52 bomber, the Stratofortress, and then dropped. At once, the X-15's rocket would burst into life and blast the plane even further, into the outer atmosphere. The X-15 flew so high and so fast that the wing flaps used to control direction on ordinary planes would have had no effect. So when the pilot moved his joystick he was actually controlling little rocket thrusters.

Top Speed

| 200 | 3400 | 6800 |

POWER
XLR99 rocket engine

LAUNCH SYSTEM
B-52 plane

TOP SPEED
4,520 mph

MACH SPEED
6.7

MAXIMUM ALTITUDE
67 miles

PILOT'S EYE VIEW

The canopy of the X-15's cockpit was largely metal and the pilot could see out only through the small windows. Only three X-15s were ever made and only one flew at any time. So, the view of the X-15 outside the window in this image shows what it would look like if two did fly together!

| 10200 | 13600 | 17000 | 4,5220 mph |

WHISTLING THROUGH THE SKIES

Painted black and shaped like a dagger to reduce its visibility to radar, the Lockheed SR-71 Blackbird was the ultimate spy plane. If it was ever spotted and shot at, its speed allowed it to outrun any missile. In fact, it was the fastest jet plane ever, able to reach 2,193.2 mph. In 1974, a Blackbird flew from New York to London in well under two hours.

Top Speed

| 200 | 3400 | 6800 |

SSH...

The Blackbird was built in secret and incorporated all kinds of advanced technology and materials. It was the first 'stealth' plane, painted with a special oxide to disguise it from radar. To cope with searing temperatures generated by friction in the upper atmosphere, it was made of 93 per cent titanium. This meant it could take operating temperatures of up to 950°F (510°C).

FINAL FLIGHT

The Blackbird was in operation from 1964 to 1998 and 32 were built. One is now in the Smithsonian Institution in Chantilly, Virginia, USA. On its last flight on 6th March 1990, pilots Lt. Col. Raymond E. 'Ed' Yielding and Lt. Col. Joseph T. 'JT' Vida set a speed record by flying from Los Angeles to Washington, D.C., in 64 minutes, averaging 2,124 mph.

POWER
Two Pratt & Whitney J58 engines

LAUNCH SYSTEM
Normal take-off

TOP SPEED
2,193.2 mph

MACH SPEED
3

MAXIMUM ALTITUDE
16 miles

PRICE
$34,000,000

10200   13600   17000   **2,193.2 mph**

FOX ON THE RUN

All of the high-speed planes featured so far were made in tiny numbers. Not the Russian MiG-25. Nearly 1,200 of them were built. Nicknamed the Foxbat, the MiG-25 was extremely rugged and functional as well as being fast. It was designed as a fighter with powerful radar to see through enemy stealth systems. But most MiG-25s were used for observation.

Top Speed	200	3400	6800

FOXED

Foxbat was the codename that NATO gave the MiG-25. They gave all fighter aircraft names beginning with F, and bombers names beginning with B. There is no such animal as a foxbat, but the word combines the cunning of a fox with the stealth of a bat. The flying fox is the world's largest bat, found in the tropical forests of Asia and Australia.

FOXBAT V BLACKBIRD

The Mikoyan Gurevich MiG-25 Foxbat was created by the Soviet Union in 1964 to combat the Blackbird – and is almost as fast. It rarely flew at its maximum speed of Mach 3.2 (2,170 mph), since the engines were likely to blow up at that speed. All the same, it could comfortably cruise at Mach 2.8 (1,900 mph). However, the Foxbat and Blackbird never met in combat.

POWER
Two Turmansky turbojet engines

LAUNCH SYSTEM
Normal take-off

TOP SPEED
2,170 mph

MACH SPEED
2.8 or (disastrously) 3.2

MAXIMUM ALTITUDE
23 miles

10200   13600   17000   **2,170 mph**

FASTER THAN SOUND

People once thought it was impossible to fly faster than sound. When planes did fly near the speed of sound, they would shake and be hard to control – so the speed of sound became known as the sound barrier. But on 14th October 1947, the Bell X-1, piloted by Chuck Yeager, broke safely through this barrier – flying faster than sound for the first time.

IT GOES BOOM!

People on the ground certainly knew Yeager had broken the sound barrier. When a plane flies very fast, it pushes up waves of pressure in the air in front, like the bow waves in front of a boat. These waves travel only at the speed of sound, but Yeager's plane was flying faster. So his plane began to scrunch them up ahead of it into one giant shock wave. Eventually, the shock wave burst like a burst paper bag, sending out a loud sound called a sonic boom.

MAKING HISTORY

The Bell X-1 was an experimental plane, powered by a rocket and shaped like a machine-gun bullet. For its historic flight, it was carried into the air beneath a B-29 bomber. Nearly four miles up, the bomber dropped the X-1. At once, Yeager fired the rocket and blasted the X-1 away. Within minutes, he had broken through the sound barrier, flying at over 700 mph!

On one flight six years after breaking the sound barrier, Yeager's plane went into a rapid, uncontrollable spin as it dived. His head was flung against the cockpit canopy, cracking its canopy. Luckily, he was able to regain control just in time.

Top Speed	200	3400	6800

POWER
Liquid-fuel rocket

LAUNCH SYSTEM
Drop launch from B-29

TOP SPEED
1,450 mph

MACH SPEED
2.24

MAXIMUM ALTITUDE
over 17 miles

| 10200 | 13600 | 17000 | 1,450 mph |

SUPERSONIC LUXURY

Nowadays, only military pilots can fly faster than sound. But between 1969 and 2003, ordinary people could beat the sound barrier, too, if they flew on the supersonic jet airliner Concorde. A normal flight from London to New York lasts up to eight hours. On Concorde, the flight was less than three and a half hours, flying at Mach 2, twice the speed of sound. But Concorde was heavy on fuel and expensive to run, and in 2003 it was withdrawn from service.

RUSSIAN RIVAL

In 1977 and 1978, Concorde briefly had an even faster rival, the Russian Tu-144, although it only flew in the Soviet Union. Both the Tu-144 and Concorde had unmistakable triangular or 'delta' wings. Delta wings are not so efficient at lifting the plane at low speeds. But at supersonic speeds they give much better stability and control than conventional wings.

Top Speed	200	3400	6800

DROOP SNOOT

To cut air resistance at supersonic speeds to a minimum, Concorde and the Tu-144 had a pencil-thin shape and a very long, pointed nose. The nose would have made it hard for the crew to see the runway, so it was designed to hinge down for take-off and landing. This was nicknamed a droop snoot.

POWER
Four Rolls-Royce/ Snecma Olympus turbojet engines

LAUNCH SYSTEM
Normal runway take-off

TOP SPEED
1,350 mph

MACH SPEED
2.04

MAXIMUM ALTITUDE
11 miles

| 10200 | 13600 | 17000 | 1,350 mph |

WHIRLING PROPELLERS

The fastest planes are shot through the air by jets and rockets. But some planes driven only by whirling propellers can really move it, too. In World War II, fighter planes such as the British Spitfire and the German Focke-Wulf Fw 190 were ripping through the skies at over 400 mph. Towards the end of the war, the American Grumman company joined in with the F8F Bearcat, the fastest-ever propeller plane.

Top Speed	200	3400	6800

GRIZZLY BEAR

Long after the war the Bearcat is still a favourite with air racers for its acrobatic ability and amazing turn of speed. In 1969, air racer Lyle Shelton found a wrecked Bearcat, lovingly rebuilt it and named it Rare Bear. In 1989, Shelton flew the 43-year-old Rare Bear at a world record speed of 528.33 mph in Los Angeles, California.

POWER
Pratt & Whitney R2800 piston engine

LAUNCH SYSTEM
Normal runway take-off

TOP SPEED
528.33 mph

MAXIMUM ALTITUDE
7.7 miles

GALLOPING MUSTANGS!

Bearcats are not the only wartime fighter planes still ripping it up in air races. Air racer Steve Hinton flies a modified P-51 Mustang dating from 1944, which he calls Voodoo. His rival is another modified P-51, Strega, flown by veteran Bill 'Tiger' Destefani. Both more than 70 years old, these planes race at speeds well over 490 mph.

10200   13600   17000   **528.33 mph**

SKY RACERS

For sheer speed and thrills, nothing can beat air racing, the world's fastest motor-sport. Right in front of spectators, some of the world's best pilots whip their planes in and out of 80-ft-high (24-m) inflatable pylons known as Air Gates. The aircraft swoop, bank, turn, roll and perform tricky manoeuvres with astonishing agility as pilots race to achieve the fastest times.

| Top Speed | 200 | 3400 | 6800 |

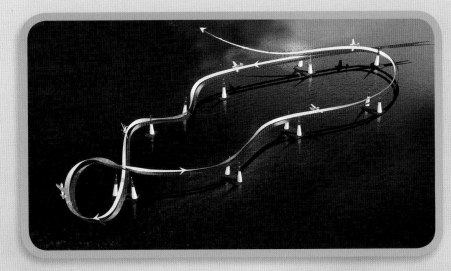

RED BULL REVELS

One of the best-known series of races is Red Bull Air Race World Championship. A course of pylons is laid out over water near a city, and 12 pilots compete by flying one by one through the pylons against the clock. They race small high-performance aerobatic planes, such as the Corvus Racer 540, with top speeds of 250–260 mph.

RENO ROARERS

At the yearly air races held at Reno in Nevada, there is a famous 'Unlimited Class' race, which any propeller-driven plane can enter. The race is dominated by modified World War II fighters that roar round the oval course at speeds of about 500 mph. In the Sport Class for home-built planes, Curt Brown hit 538 mph in his jet-engined Viper.

POWER
Lycoming piston engine

LAUNCH SYSTEM
Normal runway take-off

TOP SPEED
265 mph

CLIMB RATE
3,700 ft per minute

ROLL RATE
420° per second

10200	13600	17000	2665 mph

SUPER CHOPPER

Helicopters are wonderful for their ability to hover in mid-air and take off and land vertically. But they are not really known for their speed. That may change with the Eurocopter X^3. The Eurocopter is unofficially the world's fastest helicopter, reaching 293 mph in an early flight in 2013.

Top Speed	200	3400	6800

SPINNING FORWARD

To fly forward, an ordinary helicopter must tilt forward slightly so that the rotors pull it along. But this restricts speed. The Eurocopter gets round this limitation with a 'hybrid' approach. Besides the usual horizontal helicopter rotor, it also has two vertical 'tractor' propellers like a plane's, set on little wings. The main rotors still do all the lifting, but these extra propellers really add to the Eurocopter's forward speed.

AT THE CONTROLS

To control a helicopter, the pilot has two sticks that alter the 'pitch' or angle of the rotor blades. The 'collective' pitch control changes all the blades together. You steepen the pitch to increase lift in order to climb, and reduce it to descend. The 'cyclic' pitch control changes the pitch of the blades as they go round. Using this, the pilot can turn the helicopter in a particular direction by adding more lift at the front, back, left or right.

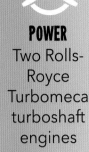

POWER
Two Rolls-Royce Turbomeca turboshaft engines

LAUNCH SYSTEM
Vertical take-off and landing

TOP SPEED
293 mph

CRUISING SPEED
253 mph

CLIMBING SPEED
1 mile per minute

10200	13600	17000	2293 mph

Bell X-1

The Bell X-1, which broke the sound barrier for the first time, was the first of the USA's X planes. X stands for experimental, and they are all one-off planes designed to try out ideas. Many were developed in top-secret conditions at Edwards Air Force in southern California. They range from the X-37 space plane to the X-49 Speedhawk helicopter. By 2012, there had been 56 X-plane projects.

Blackbird

The Lockheed SR-71 was perhaps the best spy plane ever. Not only was it astonishingly quiet inside the cab, but it was equipped with a super-sharp camera and radar so powerful that it could detect stars in broad daylight. You could even read the number plates on shots of cars on the ground taken by Blackbird's camera while the plane was flying at over 2,000 mph and 80,000 ft (24,380 m) up.

MiG-25

The MiG-25 flew during the period of the Cold War between the USA and the Soviet Union in the decades after World War II. The plane was cloaked in secrecy but American technicians learned all about it when a Soviet pilot landed his MiG-25 at Hakodate Airport, Japan, in 1976. US Air Force technicians dismantled the plane and studied it carefully, before sending all the bits back to the USSR.

P-51 Mustang

First seen in 1941, the P-51 Mustang was one of the most famous American fighter planes in World War II. With its powerful Rolls-Royce Merlin engine, it could fly at over 440 mph and outrun any of its German opponents. Its 75-gallon (285-litre) wing tanks also enabled it to fly missions lasting longer than six hours. That made it the perfect escort for bombers on long-range missions.

Red Bull races

For spectators, one of the most thrilling things about the Red Bull air races is just how close the planes come. The races are often held over rivers right in the heart of major cities such as New York, London and Budapest. The inflatable pylons or 'Air Gates' are anchored in the water, and people can watch from the nearby banks as the planes zip in and out of them.

Eurocopter X³

The Eurocoper X³ helicopter flies so fast that there are problems with the spinning rotor. Extra drag is created on the side of the rotor blade that moves forward as it rotates. And on the other side, the blade retreats so fast that it provides only a little lift to keep the helicopter in the air. So the designers of the X³ added a special 'Slowed Rotor' – a reduced rotor speed – to counteract the effect.

INDEX

GLOSSARY

A
acceleration 9
air racing 26–27, 31

B
Bell X-1 20–21, 30

C
Cessna Citation X 7
Concorde 22–23

D
Darpa Falcon HTV-2 10–11
delta wings 22

E
Eurocopter X³ 28–29, 31

F
F8F Bearcat 24–25
Foxbat 18–19

H
hypersonic 11

J
Jetman 6

L
Lockheed SR-71 Blackbird 16–17, 19, 30

M
Mach numbers 8
MiG-25 18–19, 30

P
P51 Mustang 25, 31
P51 Strega 25
private jets 7

R
Red Bull Air Race World Championship 27, 31
Rossy, Yves 6

S
scramjets 13
sound barrier 20
speed 8–9
speed guns 9
speed of sound 8, 11, 20
speedo-meters 9
stealth planes 17
supersonic 11

T
Tu-144 22, 23

U
'Unlimited Class' race 27

X
X-15 14–15
X-43A 12–13

Y
Yeager, Chuck 20

Glider An aircraft with no engine that flies using air currents

Hypersonic More than five times faster than sound

Mach number Number of times faster than sound

Scramjet A jet engine that has no fan but relies on the plane's movement at supersonic speeds to ram air into the engine

Sound barrier An imaginary barrier to exceeding the speed of sound

Sonic boom The loud boom made when a plane flies faster than sound

Stealth measures Design features and devices that help to hide a plane from enemy radar

Supersonic Faster than sound

Tractor propellers Propellers that pull an aircraft forward

THE AUTHOR

John Farndon is Royal Literary Fellow at Anglia Ruskin University in Cambridge, UK. He has written a huge number of books for adults and children on science, technology and nature, and has been shortlisted four times for the Royal Society's Young People's Book Prize.

THE ILLUSTRATORS

UK artist Mat Edwards has been drawing for as long as he can remember. He began his career with a four-year apprenticeship as a repro artist in the ceramic industry, and has been a freelance illustrator since 1992.

Jeremy Pyke left the RAF to follow his passion for illustration. He has worked on many children's books and uses oil, watercolour, computer-generated illustration and 3D animation.